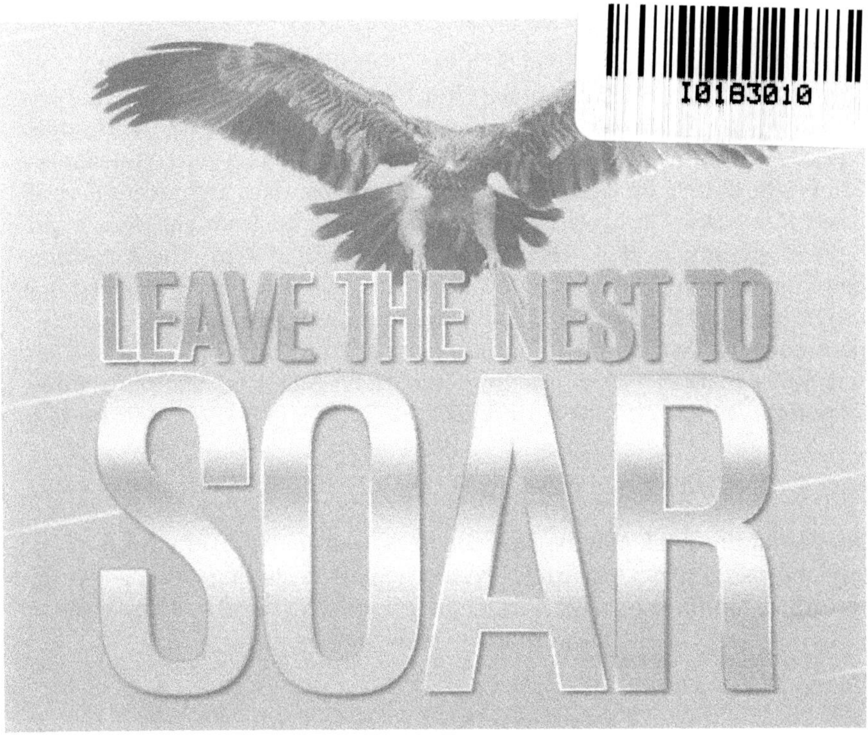

LEAVE THE NEST TO SOAR

ABIMBOLA AKINYEMI IDOWU

Syncterface Media
London
www.syncterfacemedia.com

Unless otherwise indicated, all Scripture quotations in this book are taken from the King James Version of the Holy Bible. Scriptures marked NKJV are taken from the New King James Version®. Copyright © 1982 by Thomas Nelson. Scriptures marked GWT are taken from God's Word Translation Copyright © 1995 by God's Word to the Nations. Used by permission of Baker Publishing Group. Scriptures marked AMP are from The Amplified Bible Copyright © 1954, 1958, 1962, 1964, 1965, 1987 by The Lockman Foundation. Scriptures marked NLT are from the New Living Translation, copyright © 1996, 2004, 2015 by Tyndale House Foundation. Used by permission of Tyndale House Publishers Inc., Carol Stream, Illinois 60188. Scriptures marked NASB are from the New American Standard Bible Copyright © 1960, 1962, 1963, 1968, 1971, 1972, 1973, 1975, 1977, 1995 by The Lockman Foundation
(Capitalised text and italics may be used for emphasis)

No part of this book may be reproduced or transmitted in any form or by any means, graphic, electronic, or mechanical, including photocopying, recording, taping or by any information storage or retrieval system, without the permission of the author.

LEAVE THE NEST TO SOAR
ISBN: 978-0-9933860-3-9
Copyright © September 2016
Abimbola Akinyemi Idowu
All Rights Reserved

Published in the United Kingdom by

Syncterface Media
London
www.syncterfacemedia.com
info@syncterfacemedia.com

Cover Design: Syncterface Media, London

This book is printed on acid-free paper

Contents

Dedication v

Acknowledgements vii

Comments ix

Preface xi

The Nest and You 13

Trapped In The Nest 25

Why Come Out of The Nest? 33

Who Am I and What is My Purpose? 45

Born To Soar 55

Soaring To Greater Heights 65

Empowered Lifestyle 77

Stop, Look and Listen [SLL] 85

Dedication

This book is dedicated to the many women and men who constantly struggle with challenges of life that keep them back from soaring to the great heights they are destined to reach.

May you continue to know and believe your wishes are still within your reach; don't give up, God your creator does not expect you to give up.

In His mercy, kindness and all of His provisions made available to you, you can choose to step out, explore, trust Him and be ready for your next higher level.

- Leave the Nest to Soar -

Acknowledgements

I acknowledge my gift of salvation and all other spiritual gifts from God that has been made available to me. I remember my parents who released me early in life to know the Lord. They paid for me to spend my high school summer holidays "long vacations" as known then at Scripture Union camps in the old Western Nigeria in the early 1960s.

To Pastor E. A. Adeboye, the General Overseer of the Redeemed Christian Church of God and Pastor Mrs. Folu Adeboye, for your gentle nudging to commit myself to serving the Lord.

To all my siblings, your prayers and encouragements each time we spoke was a source of strength to continue and be the greatest God created me to be.

To Pastors Tola and Kofo Odutola of Jesus House Baltimore under whom I have served since 1997. I acknowledge your teachings and life lessons learned under you.

To my children Gbemiga, Kikelomo and Opeyemi, you have been a continuous support in all that I wanted to do. My son, Olugbemiga who took time to read and edit the many drafts. I am grateful for sharing the writing gifts in your life with me.

To members of the Empowerment Forum for Women, our monthly meetings became the platform God used for me to share the series in this book. Your attendance at those meetings was a source of encouragement to keep me going, searching and listening to God for what will bless and impact your lives. I acknowledge you.

To all those who took time out to read this book and provided the reviews, Professor Bolaji Akinyemi, Pastor Funmi Obilana, Professor Folabo Soyinka-Ajayi; Pastor Jumoke Kilo, Ms. Kikelomo Idowu and Princess Adeola G. Ayoola. To all my other readers who called and encouraged me to finish the book, Pastor (Dr.) Pat McGodman, Pastor Mrs. Moji Bola-Sadipe, Ms. Mazie Coleman, Dr. Mrs Kofo Rotimi, Mrs. Diane Herron, Mrs. Saundra Jackson, Ms. Msache Mwaluko, Ms. Tannyka Coleman, Ms. Michelle Taylor and Mrs. Joy Nathan, I thank you and appreciate your immense support.

Finally, my greatest acknowledgement goes to my husband, Ayodeji. You made my comfort, my joy and the fulfillment of my goals your priority. Your constant support and gentle prodding that I have so much in me that needs to be shared and not give up, no matter the challenges. For all that you sacrificed so the best in me can come out, I wholeheartedly thank you and may God's kindness wrapped in His blessings be yours.

To all those who will read this book, I thank you for picking up this copy and also sharing its contents with others. Let us know how this has blessed you.

COMMENTS

"Powerful. Very clear in intention and perfectly sums up the focus on the content and concept of the book. It is a motivational book grounded, and justifies in Christian values and copious examples from the Bible – both New and Old Testaments. At the same time, it draws on contemporary civic examples that readers can relate to in real life. The use of 'nest' as a metaphor for complacency, and inaction, failing to take full advantage of one's God-given potentials is a powerful force, and I would say scary enough (the consequences) to immediately run out of the nest and get into action."

Professor Omofolabo Soyinka-Ajayi, Professor Emerita, University of Kansas, Lawrence, KS.

"I could not put this book down. I read it in a couple of hours and it spoke to me so much. Indeed God gave you the message."

Pastor Jumoke Kilo, Holy Ground Parish, Baltimore, MD.

"This book is relevant, functional, and real. At any point in our lives, we think we've made it, that's the beginning of our down fall. Having the Holy Spirit in our lives isn't supposed to be comfortable. He's suppose to challenge us to do more, be more and become more in all aspects of our lives.

Leave The Nest To Soar reminds me, reminds us, that leaving the nest isn't going to be easy, however what better way to do so than with the Host of Heavens by our side. When God moves us from one level to the next it's NEVER a decrease, it's ALWAYS an increase."

Kikelomo Idowu, OTR/L

"This book comes to remind us all of the awesome potential of every living soul being the pinnacle of God's ultimate creation. It is an ideal gift for college graduates who are stepping out of campus life into the real world."

Princess Adeola G. Ayoola. Author,
"Powerful Confessions for Life, Health, and Prosperity:
The Power in the Spoken Word"

"This is a down to earth book providing useful life lessons on moving forward and accomplishing greater things. The author cautions the reader of the dangers of refusing to leave the nest. The nest is a place of nurturing but failure to step out is tantamount to becoming trapped in it. This book is for anyone who is dissatisfied with status quo and desires to make a greater impact in life.

Pastor Funmi Obilana,
Senior Pastor, RCCG Living Spring Miracle Center.
Philadelphia, PA.
Author, "Electric Thrills and Chemistry".

PREFACE

Welcome to the season of visitation, favor and greater height, may the great God visit you with His favor and cause you to walk upon your high places.

The contents of this book are a compilation of 2014 monthly discussion topics held at a women group meeting, "Bridging the Divide Empowerment Forum" (EF), the spiritual arm of Seeds Healthcare Training Institute (SHTI). SHTI was started to train volunteers who will in turn go into the community and empower others to take care of their physical health. EF was then conceived to address the spiritual and emotional health of the women. It was more than a support group provides, it brought together women from different countries and age groups. The issues discussed over the years ranged from understanding the difference between the world's and God's view of women; Sacrifices of a Woman; Our young women are Pillars and Shipwrecks in the life of a Woman.

The pivotal point of each meeting was the declaration by the women the words of Selwyn Hughes (2010); "to be better and not bitter, to soar and not sink, to grow and not groan"- EF now added the following to make it a complete sentence -'on the journey to fulfill purpose'.

Each year we discuss topics that will empower the woman to stay in the positive end of the spectrum of our declaration statement. We realize it's easy to be bitter over things and experiences; it's faster to sink when we look around and see unhappy and depressing situations. We also know how groaning does not need much efforts to do and therefore at EF, we put our efforts into reminding women how we should strive at things that will make us better, things that will help us soar and those things that will constantly demonstrate growth in all that we do. All these is to fulfill the mandate for EF to help women with the words of *Jeremiah 15 verse 19* "If you return to me, I will restore you so you can continue to serve me."

The feedback and encouragement from the women at the Empowerment Forum was overwhelmingly positive as they opined that the information shared at those meetings be shared in a book with other women the world over. The 2014 series was chosen because it looked at the various aspects of the same theme, Soaring, which is in our declaration statement.

As you read this book, may the Holy Spirit move you to the realm of illumination so you can have a vivid picture of the glorious destiny God has prepared for you; may the Lord empower you to rise up and take possession of your portion in life in Jesus' mighty name. You have not picked up this book by chance; it is your time to leave the nest to soar to the greatest heights destined for you. This final product is for all to read, it's no longer gender-specific.

Each chapter ends with a "Points To Remember" section that highlights major points in the chapter. Some chapters in this book have declaration statements that have encouraged others to stay focused on getting out of the nest, seeking help to get out and taking necessary actions that brought them out of the areas of their struggles.

Some chapters have action items to assist with those baby steps you might want to take as you step out of the Nest. Don't keep it to yourself, share your experiences, bless and encourage someone else to read it.

It is a beautiful experience to leave the Nest to Soar.

Pastor (Dr.) Abimbola Akinyemi Idowu

What I am looking for is not out there; it is in me", Helen Keller

Chapter 1
THE NEST AND YOU

What is the Nest?

When we think about birds, a nest is a bed or receptacle prepared by a bird for its eggs and young ones. It is a place or a specially modified structure serving as an abode for animals at their nascent stages.

The nest could also be a familiar environment, a comfort zone, a place you are accustomed to, and a place you can navigate without difficulty or challenges. It is a place of security and safety where there is enough provision to survive. It is a place where the vision is birth, a place of self-discovery.

We have seen pictures of chicks in the nest; their mouths wide open, waiting for the mother to come back with food. It is a place of warmth and security and a place of total dependency.

After God led the children of Israel out of the Promised Land, He placed them in the nest of the wilderness for forty years. They literally lived in the 'Comfort zone' where all their needs were divinely provided by God. They did not plant; did not have to hunt for game to eat; did not dig wells for water, Jesus the Rock Himself followed them and gave them His living water. They did not need an earthly physician because the Great Physician Himself was ever present with them.

The passages from scripture detailed below exemplify the provisions a person in the Nest or Comfort zone enjoys. The Lord provided meat and bread for the children of Israel for forty years in the wilderness:

> *⁹ And Moses spake unto Aaron, Say unto all the congregation of the children of Israel, Come near before the LORD: for he hath heard your murmurings.*
>
> *¹⁰ And it came to pass, as Aaron spake unto the whole congregation of the children of Israel, that they looked toward the wilderness, and, behold, the glory of the LORD appeared in the cloud.*
>
> *¹¹ And the LORD spake unto Moses, saying,*
>
> *¹² I have heard the murmurings of the children of Israel: speak unto them, saying, At even ye shall eat flesh, and in the morning ye shall be filled with bread; and ye shall know that I am the LORD your God.*
>
> *¹³ And it came to pass, that at even the quails came up, and covered the camp: and in the morning the dew lay round about the host.*
>
> *¹⁴ And when the dew that lay was gone up, behold, upon the face of the wilderness there lay a small round thing, as small as the hoar frost on the ground.*
>
> *¹⁵ And when the children of Israel saw it, they said one to another, It is manna: for they wist not what it was. And Moses said unto them, This is the bread which the LORD hath given you to eat.*
>
> *¹⁶ This is the thing which the LORD hath commanded, Gather of it every man according to his eating, an omer for every man, according to the number of your persons; take ye every man for them which are in his tents.*
>
> *¹⁷ And the children of Israel did so, and gathered, some more, some less.*
>
> *¹⁸ And when they did mete it with an omer, he that gathered much had nothing over, and he that gathered little had no lack; they gathered every man according to his eating.*
>
> **Exodus 16:9-18**

> *³⁵ And the children of Israel did eat manna forty years, until they came to a land inhabited; they did eat manna, until they came unto the borders of the land of Canaan.*
>
> **Exodus 16:35**

He gave them water from the Rock that He provided for them for all of the forty years:

> ² Wherefore the people did chide with Moses, and said, Give us water that we may drink. And Moses said unto them, Why chide ye with me? wherefore do ye tempt the LORD?
> ³ And the people thirsted there for water; and the people murmured against Moses, and said, Wherefore is this that thou hast brought us up out of Egypt, to kill us and our children and our cattle with thirst?
> ⁴ And Moses cried unto the LORD, saying, What shall I do unto this people? they be almost ready to stone me.
> ⁵ And the LORD said unto Moses, Go on before the people, and take with thee of the elders of Israel; and thy rod, wherewith thou smotest the river, take in thine hand, and go.
> ⁶ Behold, I will stand before thee there upon the rock in Horeb; and thou shalt smite the rock, and there shall come water out of it, that the people may drink. And Moses did so in the sight of the elders of Israel.
>
> *Exodus 17:2-6*

He provided supernatural illumination for them:

> ²¹ **And the LORD went before them by day in a pillar of a cloud, to lead them the way; and by night in a pillar of fire,** to give them light; to go by day and night:
> ²² He took not away the pillar of the cloud by day, nor the pillar of fire by night, from before the people.
>
> *Exodus 13:21-22*

He divinely preserved and provided for them.

> ⁵ **And I have led you forty years in the wilderness: your clothes are not waxen old upon you, and thy shoe is not** waxen old upon thy foot.
>
> *Deuteronomy 29:5*

> ³⁷ He brought them forth also with silver and gold: and there was not one feeble person among their tribes.
>
> *Psalm 105:37*

The nest is a place of ease and divine provision, it also can be a place of refuge where you take shelter from the assault of the outside world. If care is not taken however, it can become a trap where you become caged in without the boldness to venture out. When you overstay in the nest, it may become very challenging if not impossible to adapt to the outside world where you are bound to face various issues of life whether you like it or not.

There are other situations beyond the control of the individual that makes it almost impossible to come out of the nest. In the following passage we read how some people are made eunuchs from their mother's womb, some by men and some by themselves.

> *¹² For there are eunuchs who were born thus from their mother's womb, and there are eunuchs who were made eunuchs by men, and there are eunuchs who have made themselves eunuchs for the kingdom of heaven's sake. He who is able to accept it, let him accept it."*
>
> **Mathew 19: 12 (NKJV)**

By extension, we can understand that some will need to be removed from the nest because of forces of evil has put a lid of limitation on their lives; they are unable to see and understand where they are. The Lord's intervention out of His kindness and compassionate character allows the power in His Word when spoken into the situations and when faith is exercised that the lid of limitation can be removed. If not, one remains in the nest.

It is important to recognize when it's time to move out of the nest, to identify signs of complacency and inertia and vacate. It is important to avoid staying longer than necessary or becoming locked in by circumstances and situations. The ability to recognize that it is time to leave the nest at the right moment depends on your relationship and absolute trust in God through the knowledge and understanding of the promises in His Word. The understanding propels and continues to encourage the decision to step out of the nest and apply the creative abilities endowed from God to fulfill purpose.

Right timing to come out of the nest is important in order to soar and not sink. You want to avoid coming out prematurely. The story of the Prodigal son is an example that shows when you come out prematurely, the outcome is not a good report for, instead of soaring, you start to sink.

The Prodigal son left the nest and within a short time started to struggle and was spiralling downwards instead of soaring. He left without his father's blessings and had to return to the nest. In the place of prayer, you will know when and how is the right time to step out.

Your coming out should lead to blessings/ benefits not years of struggling that leads to disappointments and in some cases failure.

The nest as you have read so far could mean or represent different things to different people. It could be a physical refuge, an emotional cave, a mental hideaway or a combination of all three. The eagle illustration demonstrates the physical nest, to move from your familiar neighborhood, town, state or country. You realize the limitations that the place of residence has placed on you, you muzzle your inner strength and, with encouragements from all around, you relocate and things start to look better with unimaginable opportunities for your best to shine through. You do not want to remain cooped up inside your place of residence. When that special day comes and you step out, that special day becomes your first day of edging out of the nest.

Is it an emotional nest you find yourself in? You realize all of a sudden you have become so emotionally attached to that person or situation. You have become so attached that you don't see how or imagine how you can survive without that person or get out of that situation; well, when you make that choice to venture out of that emotional nest, this translates to the realization and acknowledgment of your hidden qualities and, utilizing them to get out of the nest. It is not your destiny to be entrenched in the emotional nest.

Past and unpleasant experiences in life that makes it difficult to demonstrate positive emotions to others could keep one in an emotional nest. While these experiences are real, it is important to remember that staying in that emotional nest is not going to be as fulfilling as you would want. It is time to trust God and allow all that hurt and painful experiences to go. The relationship and walk with God will be in a safe space. In His Words, you find His promises of safety, He becomes the umbrella that provides the shade for you. And, if you fall again, He has promised to be by your side to pick you up again. This means, He will put you in touch with others that will be truthful, caring, protective and compassionate as He is.

Perhaps it is a mental nest and you think, 'I can' in one breath and with the next breath, you are also declaring, 'I can't.' You might have experienced failures in business, careers and relationships and perhaps you're thinking, this looks like a simple straight forward journey. You are convinced you could easily scale through, but those failed periods come back and you can't get yourself to pick up basic required tasks to try again. This will be a demonstration that you are staying in the 'I can't' mental nest. There are so many examples and scenarios but it is about you finding that mental nest that you have settled into and making the decision to leave that nest of 'I can't' to start to think and act from the 'I can' state, so you can soar.

It is important not to think the experience in the nest is always a negative one. It is not always so. As the eunuchs scenario describes, you can be born into a very rich and comfortable home, destiny helpers can assist you in achieving greater heights or, you can work your way through by choices you make. The journey of life takes us through many nests, finding out at various points in life where you are and where your next higher nest is, so you can aim at it and rise to it are the checkpoints we must all put in place.

POINTS TO REMEMBER

1. The nest could be a familiar environment, a place of security and safety where there is enough provision to survive.

2. If care is not taken however, it can become a trap where you become caged in without the boldness to venture out.

3. You do not want to remain cooped up inside your place of residence. When that special day comes and you step out, that special day becomes your first day of edging out of the nest.

4. The journey of life takes us through many nests, it is finding out at various points in life where you are and where your next higher nest is, so you can aim at it and rise to it.

ACTION ITEMS

- Identify that one thing at your physical, emotional and mental nests that you want to move out of.

- Write them down and put 'I can' beside each.

- Put a time frame of start date when you want to start and an end date. Depending on the issues / challenges or barriers, if possible make it within a 3-6 months period.

- Write specific actions/ tasks you plan to do vs. the ones you ended up doing that worked against each challenge that you overcame

- At the completion of moving out and climbing up on each issue, celebrate yourself. It is an empowering and motivating experience to see you can succeed.

- Write a declaration to help you maintain your 'I can' state of mind.

- Start to apply what has worked here to other areas of your life.

DECLARATION STATEMENT

Complete and write down what comes to your mind as the declaration statement.

"I declare I can make it if I...."

"Once I knew only darkness and stillness. My life was without past or future. But a little word from the fingers of another fell into my hand that clutched at emptiness and my heart leaped to the rapture of living", Helen Keller

Chapter 2
TRAPPED IN THE NEST

The eagle builds it's nest very high up in the tree then lines it with the softest feathers. When the eggs are hatched, she diligently takes care of her eaglets, giving them her complete and undivided attention. She provides tasty food for them every day.
After weeks of tender loving care, when she is sure it is time to start the journey to learn how to fly that is, to leave the nest and fly properly, without any warning, she pulls out the feathers that has cushioned the inside of the nest, she then proceeds to break up the twigs and eventually overturns their nice comfortable home.

Like the eaglets, we forget that there might be twigs around our nests that are being plugged out by our mother eagle so we can move out of the nest. In fact, there might be gaps in the nest that equates to cracks in the foundations of our lives, though we feel the foundation is strong and not faulty but it is not so. We continue to live each day in our current situations as if that is the best we can get.

The nest is a place to hurdle, a place of warmth, security and a comfort zone. The apparent security, provisions, loving environment or safety provided by the nest may give a false sense of security which can cause you to remain trapped in the nest while there are greater heights to be scaled outside.

In the nest, you are always a receiver, never a giver,

always waiting for a hand to feed you but the Lord is saying, there is much more out there prepared ready for you. God is nudging you to come out of the nest to experience His fullness. Like the mother eagle nudges her eaglets that it is time to learn and start flying, so the Lord by His Spirit, nudges you to get out of your comfort zone, use the gifts He has endowed you with, i.e., that of creativity, that of pulling down and building up; that of finding your way back to Him when you are lost; that of doing greater works than the Lord himself did. If you do not get out of the nest, you limit yourself and fulfilling purpose does not become a reality.

> *9 But as it is written, Eye hath not seen, nor ear heard, neither have entered into the heart of man, the things which God hath prepared for them that love him.*
>
> *1 Corinthians 2:9*

In as much as you might still be huddled in the nests, that could be, your parent's home, the familiar environment, the job you've had for years or career you are engaged in, and your perceived security and safety in those nests, you cannot reach your ultimate height in life. Remaining in those nests now becomes an entrapment.

We are created to grow, mature and become productive. The Lord is saying, there is much out there prepared for you. God is nudging you to come out of the nest and experience His fullness. He has equipped you with all that you need to step out, starting with His excellent Spirit. With each step you don't take to leave the comfort zone of the nest you have settled in—which you might have outgrown—His other resources you need to keep growing, keep soaring, might be delayed in getting to you. If only you will be fully persuaded that you have what it takes to fulfill your dreams and start to soar.

You have what it takes to be the best, trust in His spoken Words.

> ¹¹ *For I know the thoughts that I think toward you, saith the LORD, thoughts of peace, and not of evil, to give you an expected end.*
>
> ***Jeremiah 29:11***

You have what it takes to have dominion over all situations, connect to God for wisdom, strength, grace and favour concerning all areas of your life, your career, marriage, finances and your spiritual life. A relationship with God frees you from being trapped in the nest. The Lord of Glory was slain to receive all these benefits for you, hallelujah.

> ¹¹ *And I beheld, and I heard the voice of many angels round about the throne and the beasts and the elders: and the number of them was ten thousand times ten thousand, and thousands of thousands;*
>
> ¹² *Saying with a loud voice, Worthy is the Lamb that was slain to receive power, and riches, and wisdom, and strength, and honour, and glory, and blessing.*
>
> ¹³ *And every creature which is in heaven, and on the earth, and under the earth, and such as are in the sea, and all that are in them, heard I saying, Blessing, and honour, and glory, and power, be unto him that sitteth upon the throne, and unto the Lamb for ever and ever.*
>
> ¹⁴ *And the four beasts said, Amen. And the four and twenty elders fell down and worshipped him that liveth for ever and ever.*
>
> ***Revelation 5:11-14***

No matter how safe and comfortable a nest may seem, you are not designed to remain there forever. There comes a time when you must come out of the nest to soar to your next level. Just as the mother eagle will let the eaglets out of the nest suddenly, the Lord has a way of ejecting you out of the nests you have built. And, if you refuse to leave when nudged or can not perceive what is happening around you, at the appointed time, God, in order for you to experience His faithfulness and make your dreams come true, He will ensure you are pushed out of the nest. You will have the rude awakening when many uncomfortable and at times, dishonoring and disrespectful things start to happen around you and to you. It may be your final cue to leave the nest.

In *Deuteronomy 32 verse 11* the New Living Translation says, *"Like an eagle that rouses her chicks and hovers over her young, so he spread his wings to take them up and carried them safely on his pinions."* I also like the way the King James Version renders the same scripture. It states, *"As an eagle stirreth up her nest, fluttereth over her young, spreadeth abroad her wings, taketh them, beareth them on her wings."*

The Lord guided the children of Israel; He carried them on His wings as an eagle to safety. Whichever way we look at the two versions quoted, God's strategy is evident.

In the first version, He rouses the chicks, wakes them up; in the second version, it is their nest (the structural build-up) that He starts to disturb in order to catch their attention and prepare them for His own plans.

At the appointed time, the Lord orchestrates your life in such a way that there will be an awakening, a disturbance or a shaking to alert you that it is time to take the giant step of faith and come out of the nest. We must seize the opportunity once it presents itself to move ahead in life so we do not have to face the consequences of disobedience as Jonah did.

Once you begin to feel this awakening, you must carry out a personal assessment to determine where you are exactly in that phase of your life. You might find yourself in any of these four possibilities in your self-assessment of where you are and the environment around you:

- Have you settled into your comfort zone and do not want to get out?

- Do you want to get out but need some nudging, such as, new skills and information?

- Are you about to get out but fear of the unknown, or distractions from every angle hit you, causing you to postpone or delay the decision to step out of the nest?

- Are you at the decision point, determined to get out, for the nest is now too small, too uncomfortable? Have your creative abilities become a force you cannot resist? Are you ready to take the eaglets fall knowing that God is waiting to catch you and prevent you from hitting the ground so you can start to soar to your next level?

Which ever of these four possibilities speaks to your situation, it is the base point from where you want to start to reach out in going forward.

POINTS TO REMEMBER

1. In the nest, you are always a receiver, never a giver, always waiting for a hand to feed you but the Lord is saying, "there is much more out there prepared ready for you."

2. If you do not get out of the nest, you limit yourself and fulfilling purpose does not become a reality.

3. God is nudging you to come out of the nest and experience His fullness.

4. If only you will be fully persuaded that you have what it takes to fulfill your dreams and start to soar.

DECLARATION STATEMENT

"I declare I have what it takes to be the best and not be trapped in the nest. I will leave the nest and trust God's spoken words. I will be guided; if I fall God will pick me up again. I will soar."

Repeat this as often as you remember it and the power in these words will push you on in Jesus mighty name. Amen

Chapter 3
WHY COME OUT OF THE NEST?

⁶ "When we were at Mount Sinai, the LORD our God said to us, 'You have stayed at this mountain long enough.
⁷ It is time to break camp and move on. Go to the hill country of the Amorites and to all the neighboring regions—the Jordan Valley, the hill country, the western foothills, the Negev, and the coastal plain. Go to the land of the Canaanites and to Lebanon, and all the way to the great Euphrates River.

Deuteronomy 1:6-7 (NLT)

The nest as we have seen in the earlier chapters of this book has a lot of great benefits attributed to it but in spite of all these attributes, it must be said that it is also a place of limitation, a place where barriers and boundaries are set. It is meant to be a place of temporary habitation, not a place of permanent abode. When you settle into the nest, you allow yourself to become trapped. You may not intentionally want to stay trapped in the nest but these two words can summarize the experience of becoming trapped; "Comfort zone."

The Comfort zone can be the people in your life, places you are accustomed to, things and habits that have become part of you. Some are born rich; their comfort zone is their rosy lives and stable family environments. For others, it is remaining in the environment of their troubled past and the fear to venture out into the unknown that has become their 'comfort' zone. In these various scenarios, the outside world is too rough and rocky which leads them to struggle with the question, "Why should I come out of the nest?" They ask, "why not stay in the comfort of the family home? Why not continue to relate with the familiar people I am used to?"

As much as these could be troubling questions and thoughts with no easy and simple answers, it is worth highlighting some justifications to remain in the nest is the best option.

An understanding of your world view, how narrow or wide might keep you in the nest. If you grew up shielded from the true realities of life, believing it is not full of ups and downs; mountain tops and valleys with more turns and bends; more roads with bumps and potholes than smooth straight roads free of obstruction; then remaining in the nest become understandable. If you choose not to identify with changes going on around you, you will not see the need to explore, to be flexible and try something different. Staying in the nest is the best and safer option.

Your mindsets and attitudes towards people, situations and issues around could keep you in the nest. Spiritual and physical complacency could be justification we come up with why it is better and safer to remain in the nest.

However, on the flip side, there are many reasons why you should not remain in the nest. God had to intervene when the children of Israel were beginning to get comfortable after they reached Mount Sinai. He asked them to leave and move on. There comes a time when you outgrow the nest and you must surely and of necessity move out of the nest in order to get to the next level, and attain your innate and God-given purpose.

One of the reasons to come out of the nest is because, over time, we outgrow the nest.

As long as you remain in the nest, there are some heights you can never scale and your untapped potential will remain dormant in you. Although the mother eagle loves, protects and takes good care of the eaglet, she is very much aware they must be let out of the nest at a particular time for them to gain the necessary survival skills or they will not make it. She tosses them out of the nest unceremoniously not because she does not care but because she knows life holds a lot of pleasant surprises and she is getting them ready to enjoy it. She is also preparing them for the unpleasant side of life that the eaglets must be primed to go through. While mother eagle breaks up the nest and lets them loose, she is ever present, ever watchful to see when they are in danger in order to rescue them. This is the way the Heavenly Father relates with you. He wants you to step out in faith, take both small cautious and giant steps knowing that He is ever present with you to rescue you in time of the 3-Ts; Trials, Troubles and Tribulations. He also guides you with His Spirit and His Words so you do not miss your way.

> [6] *So be strong and courageous! Do not be afraid and do not panic before them. For the LORD your God will personally go ahead of you. He will neither fail you nor abandon you."*
>
> ***Deuteronomy 31:6 (NLT)***
>
> [20] *Teaching them to observe all things whatsoever I have commanded you: and, lo, I am with you always, even unto the end of the world. Amen.*
>
> ***Matthew 28:20***

There is a purpose each person on earth is created to fulfill because God is a God of purpose. We come out of the nest so we can fulfill God's purpose for our lives. He never creates anything just for the fun of it; He creates with a clear-cut mandate or purpose. One of the ways to discover that purpose and fulfill it is to get out of your nest: "the

Comfort zone." You cannot fully know your purpose for each level without hearing His voice. God still speaks but you may not hear because of the disorder and chattering environment that is the order of the day in the nest. Life is generally noisy until you move out of the crowd and spend quality time alone with God. It is then you hear His voice and know His will for your life.

> [22] And he rose up that night, and took his two wives, and his two womenservants, and his eleven sons, and passed over the ford Jabbok.
> [23] And he took them, and sent them over the brook, and sent over that he had.
> [24] And Jacob was left alone; and there wrestled a man with him until the breaking of the day.
> [25] And when he saw that he prevailed not against him, he touched the hollow of his thigh; and the hollow of Jacob's thigh was out of joint, as he wrestled with him.
> [26] And he said, Let me go, for the day breaketh. And he said, I will not let thee go, except thou bless me.
> [27] And he said unto him, What is thy name? And he said, Jacob.
> [28] And he said, Thy name shall be called no more Jacob, but Israel: for as a prince hast thou power with God and with men, and hast prevailed.
> [29] And Jacob asked him, and said, Tell me, I pray thee, thy name. And he said, Wherefore is it that thou dost ask after my name? And he blessed him there.
> [30] And Jacob called the name of the place Peniel: for I have seen God face to face, and my life is preserved.
>
> **Genesis 32:22-30**

Jacob needed an encounter with God to face his brother Esau who was coming to meet him with a large group of four hundred men. He realized he needed to move out of his Comfort zone, the house of Laban, to fulfill his own destiny. Once he summoned courage, he left his uncle's house and sent his family to the other side, leaving him alone with God. In His divine presence he had an angelic visitation that changed his life forever. He got a change of name and a change of story.

In order to fulfill purpose and come out of the nest, God's call or assignment is another reason to step out of the nest. It is a dangerous thing not to do the will of God because your disobedience to such instructions can cause other people to perish or miss their portions in life.

Responding to the call of God on your life is an adventure that requires you to journey beyond the boundaries of your nest.

The story of Jonah in *Jonah 1 verses 1 - 14* stands out as an example of what happens when God gives an assignment that requires that you leave your area of comfort. He was comfortable to stay in the physical nest of where He lived but God needed him in His agenda not to destroy the people of Nineveh because of their sins. He was sent to Nineveh but he decided to flee to Tarshish. However, like people living contrary to the plan of God for their lives, he was confronted with trial, troubles and tribulations. The boat he was travelling in got caught in a life-threatening storm. Knowing fully well that he was the cause of the predicament and to save the lives of the other people on board, Jonah asked to be thrown into the sea upon which there was a great calm.

The Lord, like the mother eagle with her watchful eyes seeking to rescue her eaglets, came to Jonah's rescue. He sent a whale that swallowed Jonah, brought him to the sea shore and dropped him there. Having learnt his lesson, Jonah then went to Nineveh to declare the word of the Lord to the people of Nineveh. They repented and were saved just because Jonah fulfilled his purpose.

When God wants to bless His children, He separates them from the crowd. He will carry them out of their usual place into another. He calls them to move out of their Comfort zone so they can fulfill their God-ordained purposes. This call carries with it an element of uncertainty and risks on one hand while absolute faith and trust in God is required to move forward. However, if a person decides to stay in his or her nest for fear of the unknown, that person inadvertently puts a lid of limitation that hinders reaching their maximum potential. It is paramount and of great relevance to leave your nest so you do not become stagnant. We need to come out of the nest so we can become an instrument and vessel for God to use in His master plan.

When God wanted to bless Abraham, the Father of faith, through whom all the nations of the world are blessed today, he was asked to get out of his Comfort zone. God asked him to move to a land He would reveal to him. That required absolute trust and faith in God. It must have been a scary thought for him to leave his father's house, take all his possessions and his wife to go to a land God promised to show him. He had no foreknowledge of where he was migrating to, there was an element of risk involved but he trusted God and became a source of blessing to the whole world. He left his nest of the known for the unknown and became very great. Generations after, we are still talking about Abraham's blessing being ours. God blesses individually but expects His blessings be shared with others.

> [1] *Now the LORD had said unto Abram, Get thee out of thy country, and from thy kindred, and from thy father's house, unto a land that I will shew thee:*
> [2] *And I will make of thee a great nation, and I will bless thee, and make thy name great; and thou shalt be a blessing:*
> [3] *And I will bless them that bless thee, and curse him that curseth thee: and in thee shall all families of the earth be blessed.*

⁴ So Abram departed, as the LORD had spoken unto him; and Lot went with him: and Abram was seventy and five years old when he departed out of Haran.
⁵ And Abram took Sarai his wife, and Lot his brother's son, and all their substance that they had gathered, and the souls that they had gotten in Haran; and they went forth to go into the land of Canaan; and into the land of Canaan they came.
⁶ And Abram passed through the land unto the place of Sichem, unto the plain of Moreh. And the Canaanite was then in the land.
⁷ And the LORD appeared unto Abram, and said, Unto thy seed will I give this land: and there builded he an altar unto the LORD, who appeared unto him.
⁸ And he removed from thence unto a mountain on the east of Bethel, and pitched his tent, having Bethel on the west, and Hai on the east: and there he builded an altar unto the LORD, and called upon the name of the LORD

Genesis 12:1-8

Looking at the life of Abraham, you can say he overstayed in the nest. He was seventy-five years old when God called him to leave his father's house. He was married and in today's language, an elderly man, it seemed he might have lived a complacent life whereas God had a greater purpose for his life.

He was created to be a channel through which the whole world, generations upon generations after him are to be blessed, yet while he stayed in the nest among his family members, not much was known of him. That is one of the dangers of overstaying in the nest and a reason why to must come out of the nest. It was the mercy and faithfulness of God that transformed Abraham from the restricted life he lived in the nest to a life of abundance and greatness that moved him to another level. We must come out of the nest in order to demonstrate to God that we truly love and trust Him with our lives through obedience to His instructions.

³¹ But those who trust in the lord will find new strength. They will soar high on wings like eagles. They will run and not grow weary. They will walk and not faint.

Isaiah 40:31

Each time you confine yourself to the Comfort zone, it becomes difficult to hear God's call. Living your calling is only possible when you are willing to obey the Master's voice and you take the risk to step out in faith. This adventure requires faith, courage and the willingness to explore and conquer new and unfamiliar territories.

Getting stuck in the nest constitutes a blockage to your calling which inevitably prevents you from seeing who you are created to be and finding out the gifts/talents you are created with. This also stops you from taking the necessary actions needed to live your calling. Mind you, your calling doesn't have to be ministerial. You can be called to work in any sphere of life, so long as you discover it, you will thrive living out that call and impacting your generation for good.

Getting out of the nest is one of the major steps towards living your God-ordained call. No matter how hard it may seem, how challenging the process may be, step out of the nest. One of the things that differentiates those who succeed in life from those who don't is, the former discover their purpose and boldly step out to fulfill it. God intends for you to have what eyes have not seen, nor ears heard, but it takes boldness on your part to step out in faith. Take mastery over your limitations, overcome the barriers and transform them into stepping-stones. Use them to climb to the heights God has prepared for you.

This chapter opens with a question of why come out of the nest? Various reasons have been presented above but the list is non-exhaustive.

This chapter ends encouraging and motivating you not to remain cuddled in the nest with all of its warmth. You must keep reminding yourself that you are not created or born to stay in the nest, it is only a place of temporary residence, a rest area at a point in life.

As a reminder, when mother eagle nudges the eaglet out of the nest or the eaglet after a number of attempts finally experiences the first scary free fall of leaving the nest, the mother eagle hovers around watching, waiting to catch the eaglet before it hits the ground and return it back to the safety of the nest. So are we, when we take those baby steps and venture out to explore what is out there and try the uncharted paths of a career, school, relationship, business, and ministry and get discouraged because things don't go the way we thought, hoped or wished it should.

Remember, God is watching so He can pick you up again and again so you can keep trying. He has promised that when you fall, you must rise up again. Are you reading this book right now and feel there is no way to get back up, or you are thinking of trying something you have not done before that might actually take you to another level, well, pinch yourself and declare, 'I can do this; I can make that call to ask for information that I need'. The good news is, God has positioned destiny helpers along the way to hold your hands and show you the way to go; helpers that will invest in you and believe in you.

The best that God has for you is not only to get out of the nest, but also to soar and keep soaring to greater heights. You didn't stumble upon this book per chance or by mistake, it's meant to either nudge you forward in life or, to provide an answer to a friend who is stuck in life.

The most straightforward answer to the question raised in this chapter is; it is God's instruction as shown in the opening reference for this chapter and repeated below, to come out of the nest. I pray you will obey this day.

> [6] "When we were at Mount Sinai, the LORD our God said to us, 'You have stayed at this mountain long enough.
> [7] It is time to break camp and move on. Go to the hill country of the Amorites.......
>
> ***Deuteronomy 1: 6-7***

POINTS TO REMEMBER

1. There comes a time when you outgrow the nest and you must surely and of necessity move out of the nest in order to get to the next level.

2. He (God) never creates anything just for the fun of it; He creates with a clear-cut mandate or purpose.

3. Responding to the call of God on your life or discovering and fulfilling your God-given purpose is an adventure that requires you to journey beyond the boundaries of your nest.

4. Each time you confine yourself to the comfort zone, it becomes difficult to hear God's call.

5. God intends for you to have what eyes have not seen, nor ears heard, but it takes boldness on your part to step out in faith.

ACTION ITEMS

- Make a table notation in your journal with today's date and the self-assessment you come up with.

- Beside each item you identify as the area you seek to improve or move to another level

- Write beside it some baby steps you want to take to initiate the move out of the nest.

- With each baby step you take, appreciate God and celebrate the new mindset and attitude that 'You Can'.

Chapter 4
WHO AM I AND WHAT IS MY PURPOSE?

These are questions that people are constantly asking in order to understand themselves, to answer the who, what and why questions of life. Some people quickly formulate answers to the questions above with relative ease, and consequently walk in the contentment that they know. To others, the questions of "my purpose" and "who am I" nag at them as they don't have a clue about their identity. No matter what end of the spectrum you think you are on, one thing is for sure, with God and in Him, you are a very important person who He needs. He spoke concerning the children of Israel as soon as they came out of Egypt:

> [3] *Then Moses went up to God, and the LORD called to him from the mountain and said, "This is what you are to say to the descendants of Jacob and what you are to tell the people of Israel:*
> [4] *'You yourselves have seen what I did to Egypt, and how I carried you on eagles' wings and brought you to myself.*
> [5] *Now if you obey me fully and keep my covenant, then out of all nations you will be my treasured possession. Although the whole earth is mine,*
> [6] *you will be for me a kingdom of priests and a holy nation.' These are the words you are to speak to the Israelites."*
>
> ***Exodus 19: 3-6 (NIV)***

You might feel you are content in your current spot - the nest – and it's where you are supposed to be. But, we see here that God did not allow His children to stay in the same spot, to stay in slavery. No matter the limitations around you, when you allow God, He will carry you on eagles' wings as He did for the children of Israel long ago.

He will make things become easier for you as the heavens smile on you, through destiny helpers, uncommon favours and promotions.

> *⁹ But ye are a chosen generation, a royal priesthood, an holy nation, a peculiar people; that ye should shew forth the praises of him who hath called you out of darkness into his marvellous light;*
>
> *1 Peter 2:9*

According to the Word of God in *1 Peter 2 verse 9*, you are a chosen one; you are royalty (born to rule); a unique person; you are created to show forth the praises of God who called you out of darkness and out of obscurity into His marvellous light. If a person understands the revelation behind these words, his destiny will be settled forever. God is a God of purpose and plan, so if you are chosen of God, you are chosen for a specific function on earth. It means you are not a product of accident. You are on this earth to accomplish an agenda item in the divine plan of God. There is something special about your life and destiny. You are not created to remain in obscurity; you are made to shine and show forth the praises of God. No one can cover the glory of the sun, as such; no one can stop you from coming out of obscurity into the marvellous light of God except yourself. The sun never remains in the background, when the sun shines, all eyes see it, in the same vein, you cannot remain in the nest, and you must come out to soar.

Joseph was born to deliver his generation from famine and the doom it would have caused all of humanity. He came into the world with a mandate, he was a saviour and a precursor of Jesus. Despite the evil orchestrated by his brothers, under the influence of Satan, they came together against him, despite the attack of the wife of Potiphar, despite the time he spent in prison, he still fulfilled destiny. God protected his destiny all the way until it was fulfilled. God made him the ruler in a strange land so he could fulfill his purpose. When the famine eventually came, through the divine wisdom of God bestowed on him, he was able to avert the extermination of the people of his time and God's special possessions: the children of Jacob.

Purpose Discovery

Purpose discovered leads to a fulfilled life. It is a dangerous thing to be on this earth without knowing what your mission is. The reason why most people cannot leave the nest to soar, why they cannot move ahead in life is because they have no idea who they are or what their purpose is. Purpose discovered is the engine that drives the fulfillment of destiny. Discovering your purpose reveals your mission: the revelation of mission produces the vision; the vision then spurs you to action; and, the actions taken will bring about the fulfillment of the purpose.

Once we discover our purpose, we can no longer be caged; we become fired up to break away from every barrier in order to fulfill the purpose discovered. The nest becomes too small, very uncomfortable and we come to the realization that it is time to leave the nest.

Our Lord Jesus Christ came to this world with a mandate to destroy the works of the devil, set the captives free and give us abundant life. He endured suffering, shame and reproach because He was on a mission. He did not allow circumstances and situations to distract, disrupt nor deter Him from fulfilling His mission.

> [18] *The Spirit of the Lord is upon me, because he hath anointed me to preach the gospel to the poor; he hath sent me to heal the brokenhearted, to preach*

deliverance to the captives, and recovering of sight to the blind, to set at liberty them that are bruised,

Luke 4:18

⁸ He that committeth sin is of the devil; for the devil sinneth from the beginning. For this purpose the Son of God was manifested, that he might destroy the works of the devil.

1 John 3:8

Death and the grave could neither swallow our Lord Jesus up nor could it hold Him captive. He overcame death and the grave; He came out victorious, He accomplished His purpose and so could you.

John the Baptist came into this world with a special mandate to announce the coming of the Messiah. His mission was clearly stated to his parents by Angel Gabriel right before his birth. Even in his mother's womb, the unborn John the Baptist had cognizance of his purpose. When Mary, the mother of Jesus, came to visit Elizabeth, the mother of John the Baptist, the two unborn children, in their mothers' wombs nonetheless, had a connection. Mary came into the house and the anointing of God came upon John the Baptist who leapt for joy in his mother's womb to acknowledge the King of kings, our Lord and Saviour Jesus. Elizabeth prophesied over Mary and her child because she contacted the anointing that was upon the child in her womb.

⁸ And it came to pass, that while he executed the priest's office before God in the order of his course,

⁹ According to the custom of the priest's office, his lot was to burn incense when he went into the temple of the Lord.

¹⁰ And the whole multitude of the people were praying without at the time of incense.

¹¹ And there appeared unto him an angel of the Lord standing on the right side of the altar of incense.

¹² And when Zacharias saw him, he was troubled, and fear fell upon him.

13 But the angel said unto him, Fear not, Zacharias: for thy prayer is heard; and thy wife Elisabeth shall bear thee a son, and thou shalt call his name John.
14 And thou shalt have joy and gladness; and many shall rejoice at his birth.
15 For he shall be great in the sight of the Lord, and shall drink neither wine nor strong drink; and he shall be filled with the Holy Ghost, even from his mother's womb.
16 And many of the children of Israel shall he turn to the Lord their God.
17 And he shall go before him in the spirit and power of Elias, to turn the hearts of the fathers to the children, and the disobedient to the wisdom of the just; to make ready a people prepared for the Lord.

Luke 1:8-17

John the Baptist stepped out of the comfort of his home to leave in the wilderness to fulfill his assignment. He focused, as exemplified by the type of life he lived and the work he did to prepare the way of the Messiah. People did not understand him, some even criticized him but that did not deter him from focusing on his purpose. He not only prepared the way for the Lord but he was the vessel chosen to baptize the Lord after which the Holy Ghost descended upon the Lord Jesus with mighty anointing to accomplish His mission.

13 Then cometh Jesus from Galilee to Jordan unto John, to be baptized of him.
14 But John forbad him, saying, I have need to be baptized of thee, and comest thou to me?
15 And Jesus answering said unto him, Suffer it to be so now: for thus it becometh us to fulfil all righteousness. Then he suffered him.
16 And Jesus, when he was baptized, went up straightway out of the water: and, lo, the heavens were opened unto him, and he saw the Spirit of God descending like a dove, and lighting upon him:
17 And lo a voice from heaven, saying, This is my beloved Son, in whom I am well pleased.

Matthew 3:13-17

The story of John the Baptist is one of the prominent stories in the Bible because he recognized his purpose and walked in it not allowing anything to distract and deter him from his God ordained mission.

To rise up and soar, you must push away defeatist thoughts so you can discover your purpose and do all that is humanly possible while relying on the help of the Holy Spirit to fulfill it. You will also learn along the way that there are some things that only God can do in your life even in situations when you do not ask Him to do it. For He loves you, and wants you to experience His mercy and kindness.

May you hear the voice of the Lord expressly as you seek His face for the discovery of that purpose according to His promise in the book of *Isaiah 30 verse 21*, *"And thine ears shall hear a word behind thee, saying, This is the way, walk ye in it, when ye turn to the right hand, and when ye turn to the left."*

Develop that relationship with the Lord that makes it easy to know when He says it's time to leave for a larger and better nest. When you obey, He provides directions of where and what you need to fulfill His divine purpose for your life.

You may be reading this book and looking at the physical things around you, typically, age, your gender, or level of education and be discouraged but do not allow these to cripple you into remaining in the nest. His Word says, the harvest is plenty but the workers are few. There's something He has deposited in you that is still dormant that needs to wake up. There's something to stir up a passion in you if you allow the Spirit of God to help so you can fly or climb out of the nest. When you know who the Spirit of God is, it will be easy to grant Him access so

He could assist you. How? you might ask.

The Ministry of The Holy Spirit

The Holy Spirit is the Spirit of the living God, the third person in the Trinity. For believers and non-believers in our Lord Jesus Christ, this is very challenging for people to grasp.

We meet Him at the beginning;

> *¹ In the beginning God created the heavens and the earth.*
> *² The earth was formless and empty, and darkness covered the deep waters. And the Spirit of God was hovering over the surface of the waters.*
>
> ***Genesis 1:1-2 (NLT)***

We read in the anointing of Saul to become King over Israel, Prophet Samuel declared the following about the HOLY SPIRIT:

> *⁵ "When you arrive at Gibeah of God, where the garrison of the Philistines is located, you will meet a band of prophets coming down from the place of worship. They will be playing a harp, a tambourine, a flute, and a lyre, and they will be prophesying.*
> *⁶ At that time the Spirit of the LORD will come powerfully upon you, and you will prophesy with them. You will be changed into a different person.*
>
> ***1 Samuel 10:5-6 (NLT)***

The Spirit of God was very active also from the beginning to the end of the life of our Lord Jesus, so, Jesus could fulfill purpose as He is God that appeared in human flesh. As Joseph thought of getting out of the engagement with Mary, the angel spoke in *Matthew 1 verse 20*, *"For the child within her was conceived by the Holy Spirit."*

At the beginning of the ministry of Jesus, as John the Baptist finished baptizing our Lord Jesus, the bible records in *Matthew 3 verse 16* (NLT), *"After his baptism, as*

Jesus came up out of the water, the heavens were opened, and he saw the Spirit of God descending like a dove and settling on him."

In *Matthew 4 verse 1*, we saw that Jesus was led by the Spirit of God out of His comfort zone into the wilderness for a time of separation and preparation to face the perpetrator of the tests, trials and tribulations He would face while on earth. In the 2005-updated version of Lester Sumrall's, "*The Gifts and Ministries of the Holy Spirit*" we read about the ministry "Jesus performed on this earth was directed, guided and energized by the Holy Spirit."

So, when you know and walk, hear and obey His voice, you will receive the same power of the Spirit to move out of the nest. How do I know this you may ask? As you read the following two references, I pray you will receive the knowledge and understanding.

> [11] *The Spirit of God, who raised Jesus from the dead, lives in you. And just as God raised Christ Jesus from the dead, he will give life to your mortal bodies by this same Spirit living within you.*
>
> **Romans 8:11**

The promise of our Lord Jesus to send the Holy Spirit back to remain with us and in us was fulfilled in this second reference.

> [4] *And everyone present was filled with the Holy Spirit and began speaking in other languages, as the Holy Spirit gave them this ability.*
>
> **Acts 2:4**

The Holy Spirit when we allow Him starts to make the impossible things to become possible for us. Saul was changed to a different person when he encountered the Holy Spirit. It might not be comfortable initially when you encounter the Spirit of God as you are not ready to let go your will or doing things your way. The Spirit of God wants to start a relationship so you can begin to trust Him. With this new relationship, the right choices that will lead you out of one nest into a higher one become possible. The Spirit of God can be the one that is ruffling your nest in order to move you out of your comfort zone to work and fulfill purpose. When you accept our Lord Jesus as your master and saviour, you humble yourself to accept your mistakes, faults and wrong doings and ask for God's mercies to forgive you. When you accept God's gift of forgiveness and your confession about the Son, the gift of salvation and gift of His Spirit is sent back to you. The Spirit shines His light on you and the darkness around you so you can see you have been in a nest for too long. You receive understanding of other creative abilities in you that have not been tapped into and all of a sudden the light bulb goes off and you want to leave the nest and start the journey to move to a higher level.

You are not a mistake, you have been sent down to this world from the loins of God for an assignment, which is your purpose. God protected the destiny of Joseph and he fulfilled purpose to save the nation of Israel out of the impending years of famine. One of the benefits of stepping out of the nest to fulfill purpose is empowerment from above. When the Lord gets you to leave the nest and commissions you to fulfill purpose, He empowers regardless of where you are called to serve; be it in the secular or the spiritual field, the anointing for exploits is released upon your life by the Spirit of God that is within you.

POINTS TO REMEMBER

1. No matter the limitations around you, when you allow God, He will carry you on eagles' wings as He did for the children of Israel.

2. You are on this earth to accomplish an agenda item in the grand and divine plan of God.

3. The sun never remains in the background, when the sun shines, all eyes see it, in the same vein, you can't remain in the nest, and you must come out to soar.

4. The reason why most people can't leave the nest to soar, why they can't move ahead in life is because they have no idea who they are or what their purpose is.

5. Once a person discovers his purpose, he can no longer be caged or confined into a nest; he is fired up to break away from every barrier in order to fulfill the purpose.

DECLARATION STATEMENT:
"I declare….."

Chapter 5
BORN TO SOAR

²⁸ And God blessed them, and God said unto them, Be fruitful, and multiply, and replenish the earth, and subdue it: and have dominion over the fish of the sea, and over the fowl of the air, and over every living thing that moveth upon the earth.

Genesis 1:28

At creation when God blessed man, He gave him authority and dominion overall His creation. Every human created by God is wired to excel, succeed and dominate. No matter what is going on in your life, no matter your circumstance and situation, no matter the environment you live in, you have all it takes to rule and be in absolute control of the events of your life. It is not this straight forward for everyone, distractions in life can make it that the God-given control is not activated, but the wiring is already laid.

This is so when you remember that like an eagle, you are created to soar, you are not expected to remain in your nest or comfort zone forever. The Lord made a divine provision for you when He sent His only begotten Son, our Lord and Saviour Jesus Christ to take your place and die for your sins so you can be free to enter into the fullness of God's goodness for the resources are already made available to you.

Our Lord Jesus Christ laid down His life so we can receive power, riches, wisdom, strength, honor, glory and blessing. All these benefits accrue at redemption. You are fully loaded to succeed, so there is no excuse for you not to leave the nest to soar. You are endowed with all it takes to make it happen. Get up, step out ready to leave the nest to soar.

> [8] When the Most High divided to the nations their inheritance, when he separated the sons of Adam, he set the bounds of the people according to the number of the children of Israel.
> [9] For the LORD's portion is his people; Jacob is the lot of his inheritance.
> [10] He found him in a desert land, and in the waste howling wilderness; he led him about, he instructed him, he kept him as the apple of his eye.
> [11] As an eagle stirreth up her nest, fluttereth over her young, spreadeth abroad her wings, taketh them, beareth them on her wings:
> [12] So the LORD alone did lead him, and there was no strange god with him.
> [13] He made him ride on the high places of the earth, that he might eat the increase of the fields; and he made him to suck honey out of the rock, and oil out of the flinty rock;
> [14] Butter of kine, and milk of sheep, with fat of lambs, and rams of the breed of Bashan, and goats, with the fat of kidneys of wheat; and thou didst drink the pure blood of the grape.
>
> ***Deuteronomy 32:8-14***

The Lord our God like the mother eagle cares for you; He has prepared all things necessary for you to soar to the heights He destined you to reach. He has made available all the financial, material, spiritual and emotional provisions you need to succeed, you are complete in Him and His Spirit is ever present to guide and instruct you all the way.

With all the blessings bestowed on you by our Lord, you are to soar to creative living, self- acceptance, positive change and victorious faith in every aspect of your life.

However, for you to climb and rise to your designated heights having also found your purpose in life, you should find time to do a personal self-assessment to know if you are in a physical, mental or emotional nest. What are the things that represent the nest in your life; that is, the comfort zone that you have settled into? Why have you remained in the nest? What are the things holding you back from leaving the nest? What gifts do you have that when used will lift you to your next level? What are the actions, small or big, you must take to break away from the nest to soar like the eagle?

Ruth had to leave the physical, emotional and mental nests in her life to soar and be counted in the lineage of our Lord Jesus Christ. The bible narrates how she had to leave her people, her culture, her way of thinking and follow Naomi her widowed mother-in-law. She seemed to have been more concerned about taking care of her mother-in-law, the choice she made to follow Naomi opened the opportunity of greater and higher connection through Boaz that ensured her rise to the level of her name listed in the genealogy of our Lord Jesus.

We must remember the compassionate virtue in Ruth which spurred her to consider the loneliness that Naomi will face in her old age in the absence of her husband and sons. She demonstrated kindness and sensitivity to the needs of others.

The story of Ruth stands as an example of one who made the conscious decision to step out of the nest into the unknown. We could make some conjectures that she perceived the family of her late husband had something that was different. She was not completely sure of what will happen to her but she was determined to leave, she said "wherever you go I will go and your God will be my God". You may not completely know what the future holds (which we don't as humans with finite minds), but you are ready to trust in God who will guide your paths and the decisions you make.

The story of Esther demonstrates clearly that working in God's plan will cause you to step out of the nests you might think you are confined into. Esther had to step out of being 'Hadassah', the Jewish slave, to soar to the position of the great King Xerxes favoured queen. A closer look at Esther showed how she left the nest, the comfort and safety of Mordecai's house where she was raised.

Esther was nudged out of the nest on at least two occasions in order for her to fulfill purpose. Mordecai, her uncle was instrumental at both times. First, he got her to go to the palace and be one of the young ladies to be groomed to appear before the king. The second time, her uncle had to remind her if she doesn't step out of the nest, the comfort zone of being a queen, her own life was at stake. She had to step out of that nest to do the unthinkable, appearing before the king without being invited. Esther did, and the result was she saved the lives of many people, the young and old Jews from slaughter.

A further look at Esther shows as stated earlier, she left the physical, emotional and mental nests in her life and soared to the following heights:

- Twice the scepter of favor was held out to her (*Esther 5:2;8:4*)

- Twice the King promised her "even if it is half of his kingdom" (*Esther 5:6;7:2*)

- Mordecai and Queen Esther decreed the Festival of Purim. *Esther 9 verse 32, "So the command of Esther confirmed the practices of Purim, and it was all written down in the records."(NLT)*.

This is an indication that her full royal and legal authority backed the two decrees written by Mordecai. The first to save the Jews from being killed by other people in the 127 provinces of the kingdom of King Xerxes; the second, established the annual celebration of the Festival of Purim. Esther soared because she left the comfort zone of the nests she knew and flew on the wings of favour. As you read this, I pray you will also soar to greater heights on the wings of favour of God in your situation.

You can see that in life, other people might be in your business and you want to resist them, ignore them or even fight them, be watchful, God might be using them to nudge or force you out of your nests so you can impact your generation for good.

Abigail was in a comfortable nest, she was married to Nabal, wealthy man with flocks, shepherds and a large household. Her household was comfortable for she was able to easily lay hold of 200 loaves of bread, 200 fig cakes, 100 clusters of raisins, two wine skins full of wine, 5 sheep and lots of grains. She assessed the situation, had an understanding of the implications of her husband's response to David's appeal for food and her quick action saved the household of Nabal. She soared to the next level becoming a queen to King David the anointed of God, and she was in the lineage of our Lord Jesus, by one small act. The gift of wisdom in her, the decision to respond to the request of David and the action she took propelled her to the next level.

The story of another lady resonated and was relevant to the monthly meeting topics. Helen Keller's story is so inspiring that despite the loss of her sight and hearing abilities at a very young age of 19 months that could have kept her in the nest of her parents' home, she left that nest.

Her disabilities did not keep her in the nest. According to Wikipedia, she was the deaf/blind person to receive a Bachelor of Arts degree. She became an author, an educationist, a political activist and a great performer. She travelled the world over, performing and inspiring others to step out of their nests to soar despite the disabilities they might have. She had the provisions from a rich family but also a supporting teacher, Ann Sullivan and other great people of influence who nudged her on in her development.

Many other women or even men, have found themselves not moving out or making the effort to leave the nest due to many reasons (real or unreal) and issues they perceive as immovable mountains.

The journey of life however continues till you get to the point in life or the place of awakening to the realization of your full potential as you pursue the fulfillment of your purpose. Until then, it is a life of wandering in the desert, a life with lids of limitation thrust upon you. Others will give it various names or label you as not been focused, as 'jack of all trade'. The challenge others can't see might be your inability to get out of the nest even though it is uncomfortable for you.

God will protect your destiny. He will change rules for you in order to fulfill His mandate for your life and soar to levels destined for you.

I work at a community-based program with six health focus areas, supervised by a Project Director. I was employed to be in charge of one of the focus areas. It was not challenging enough for me but after 4 years of full time graduate school for a doctoral degree, the job was a way of getting out of the nest of unemployment. I envisioned it will be a short stint, it was not to be so and this year, 2016, marks 9 plus years at the job.

In the first couple of years at the job, I worked hard to develop my assigned focus area and ultimately one of my mini projects won a national award for the County. I felt very comfortable in the one area of focus I was tasked to work in. The area of focus was STI/HIV, a stigmatized condition but my passion drove me to want everyone and anyone that will listen know that the virus responsible for the infection was still very much alive. I later settled into the tasks of routine testing and invitations to speak at events. I started to feel comfortable that I knew the subject area like the back of my hand. I settled into the nest of that one focus area, coped with the secondary stigma typical for people working in the area of HIV/AIDS. Some people could not understand why I want to sustain awareness for a disease that is classified as chronic and no longer classified as infectious.

However, about seven years at the job, the Project Director left and due to the position requirements, the position was left open for some months. I couldn't apply because I didn't meet one of the critical requirements of the position. After months, the County 'miraculously' removed the stumbling block requirement that stood in my way. God used my colleagues and family members to nudge me and encourage me to apply, thereby getting me out of the nest, the comfort zone that I had created for myself. I did and the rest is history. I had become comfortable in the nest of one focus area within the program but for the past three years I now provide fiscal and program management to all six focus areas as Project Director. I moved out of the small nest of one focus area and moved to a 'larger' nest of managing six areas. This is one of a few examples of soaring to another level that I've been blessed to experience in life. I am a foreigner in the land as Joseph was in Egypt but God nudged me out of the small nest to a larger one, which is a climb into another level. He will do the same for you and you will experience a soaring to the next level of what He has planned for you in Jesus name.

May the Lord empower you to take the step of faith, leap over the wall and step out of the nest in the mighty name of Jesus.

POINTS TO REMEMBER

1. Every human created by God is wired to excel, succeed and dominate.

2. You are fully loaded to succeed, so there is no excuse for you not to leave the nest to soar.

3. With all the blessings bestowed on you by our Lord, you are to soar to creative living, self-acceptance, positive change and victorious faith in every aspect of your life.

4. The challenges that others can't see might be your inability to get out of the nest even though it is uncomfortable for you.

5. Seek to know the actions you must take to break away from the nest to soar like the eagle.

6. God will protect your destiny. He will change rules for you in order to fulfill His mandate for your life.

"Optimism is the faith that leads to achievement. Nothing can be done without hope and confidence" Helen Keller

Chapter 6
SOARING TO GREATER HEIGHTS

> *³¹ But those who trust in the LORD will find new strength.*
> *They will soar high on wings like eagles.*
> *They will run and not grow weary.*
> *They will walk and not faint*
>
> **Isaiah 40:31 (NLT)**

It is the desire of God to see all His children reach their goals in life. As you might have discovered in earlier chapters, God has made provisions for all our needs to help us reach our goals. The question is how high do you want to soar? We remember the eagle soars the farthest and the highest above all other birds, so for you to soar to greater heights, you want to understand some conditions in order to fulfil your destiny. The eagle soars to the highest levels not only by flapping its wings — this only gets it but so far — but by gliding and tilting its wings to allow for the thrust upwards that it needs to propel higher. So it is with you. In order to soar higher than others, there are some essential spiritual and natural conditions that should be in place through God's provisions if you allow Him to do it.

HIS SPIRIT: He starts by filling you with His Spirit. The role of the Spirit of God in fulfillment of purpose was discussed earlier. This section provides further examples of what happens when the Spirit of God guides you to do incredible things and moves you from one level to the other, from a small nest to a larger nest as you keep soaring higher.

Look at what the bible says during the building of the sanctuary in *Exodus 31 verses 1-5*.

> ^{1} Then the LORD said to Moses,
> ^{2} "See, I have chosen Bezalel son of Uri, the son of Hur, of the tribe of Judah,
> ^{3} and I have filled him with the Spirit of God, with wisdom, with understanding, with knowledge and with all kinds of skills—
> ^{4} to make artistic designs for work in gold, silver and bronze,
> ^{5} to cut and set stones, to work in wood, and to engage in all kinds of crafts.
>
> **Exodus 31:1-5 (NIV)**

In the story about the building of the sanctuary in *Exodus 36 verse 1*, we read how God gave the workmen *"Bezalel, Aholiab and every wisehearted man, in whom God put wisdom and understanding to know how to work all manner of work for the service of the sanctuary, according to all that the LORD had commanded."*

To climb to greater heights you want to thirst for the relationship with the Spirit that you received through acceptance of our Lord Jesus as your Lord and Savior. With His Spirit you will be able to apply the skill you have learnt, no matter how crude or simple it might seem. When His blessings are on the final product, what looks crude and simple becomes a hot item that sells beyond your expectation.

The creative nature of God in you comes with the ability to produce different things, taking ideas and transforming them into reality. God puts His seal on your creativity with wisdom and understanding and instructs you on how to go forward with an idea, on who to speak to or connect with, or who will help open the door to market the product; or assist you to re-launch your abandoned ministry.

There are other factors and practices that are of relevance

as you focus and keep your eyes on soaring higher. Let's examine the following:

Being Mindful of Your Thoughts

According to *Selwyn Hughes (2001)*, you must be "ocean-minded" and not "creek-minded"; you are to think big and not little. This is exemplified in the scripture that states,

> [7] *For as he thinketh in his heart, so is he:*
>
> *Proverbs 23:7*

The mind is one of the most powerful tools that we possess. Everything that manifests in the physical form is conceived from our thoughts. When you process an idea in your mind, a mental picture is formed. This picture registers and takes root. It becomes a driving force that galvanizes the push and passion to pursue the idea to reality.

When God spoke to Abraham about making him the father of nations when Abraham was well stricken with age and childless, God knew Abraham needed a tangible substance to keep his faith alive. He asked Abraham to step out of his tent, look at the sky and count the stars. It was a starry night and God told him that his descendants would be as numerous as the stars he saw in the sky.

> [1] *After these things the word of the LORD came unto Abram in a vision, saying, Fear not, Abram: I am thy shield, and thy exceeding great reward.*
> [2] *And Abram said, LORD God, what wilt thou give me, seeing I go childless, and the steward of my house is this Eliezer of Damascus?*
> [3] *And Abram said, Behold, to me thou hast given no seed: and, lo, one born in my house is mine heir.*
> [4] *And, behold, the word of the LORD came unto him, saying, This shall not be thine heir; but he that shall come forth out of thine own bowels shall be thine heir.*

> *⁵ And he brought him forth abroad, and said, Look now toward heaven, and tell the stars, if thou be able to number them: and he said unto him, So shall thy seed be.*
> *⁶ And he believed in the LORD; and he counted it to him for righteousness.*
>
> **Genesis 15:1-6**

That experience must have made a powerful impression in the mind of Abraham, the image was permanently engraved in his mind so much so that the Bible, in *Romans 4 verses 20-21*, records that, *"He staggered not at the promise of God through unbelief; but was strong in faith, giving glory to God and being fully persuaded that, what he had promised, he was able also to perform."*

Abraham could not entertain any doubt because he had a mental picture that was vividly painted for him. Our thoughts and minds must be right for us to rise to the level God wants us to attain. We must jealously guard our hearts so that the devil does not plant his evil thoughts of fear, or our past experiences of failure in our minds to distract us from soaring to the next level and achieve God's purpose.

We must be mindful of our thoughts knowing they could originate from God, Satan and our minds (*Selwyn Hughes, 2001*). Knowing who is behind your thoughts is of essence as you receive and process information that takes you to your next level. It is often said that the most valuable treasures are hidden from plain view. Pearls are hidden within oysters, diamonds are buried deep within the earth and gold nuggets are concealed in the heart of the great mountains. The thoughts that come from God are sometimes so challenging that we have a tendency to ignore and push them right out of our minds. God carefully and quietly hides His most precious gifts so we may experience the joy of discovering them (*Selwyn*

Hughes, 2001).

> ² It is the glory of God to conceal a thing: but the honour of kings is to search out a matter.
>
> ***Proverbs 25:2***

Embrace your God-directed thought, don't push them away because your brain says it is too challenging. As children of God, we should trust Him to lead us to those who will help us discover our purpose and soar. His promise is to make a way where there is no way. He said, He will make a way in the wilderness, He will lead the blind Israel to a path they have not gone before.

> ¹⁶ I will lead blind Israel down a new path,
>   guiding them along an unfamiliar way.
> I will brighten the darkness before them
>   and smooth out the road ahead of them.
> Yes, I will indeed do these things;
>   I will not forsake them.
>
> ***Isaiah 42:16 (NLT)***

God will shine His light over every idea in your mind that will transform you, your relationship, service, careers, business and family when you understand that the end of the idea is not only to bless you but that more people will benefit when you pursue that idea. Don't look back at hurdles you successfully jumped over, look forward to heights you are soaring to reach (*Selwyn Hughes*).

> ⁶² And Jesus said unto him, No man, having put his hand to the plough, and looking back, is fit for the kingdom of God.
>
> ***Luke 9:62***

Breaking up old patterns of thought everyday by doing something you have never done before is a strategy that has made a difference and pushed people into new levels (*Selwyn Hughes, 2001*). In the same vein, you can apply this to when you make a break with routines that do not challenge you to be creative. You must reject fear, believe more and trust more.

The other strategy recommended as helpful practice is to "keep a mental and spiritual wastebasket and discard of old ideas, throwing away the bad to get the good, the good to get the better and the better to get the best" (*Selwyn Hughes, 2001*). It is constantly working to keep your brain active, challenge it to work as it should to help you get excited about reaching out for new things.

Your total surrender to Christ and walking the journey of your life with Him will lead you into the realization and understanding of what has been deposited in you to take you to where He wants you to be.

Action Items:

- Write down at least three thoughts/ideas that keep coming up in your mind as instructed in Habakkuk 2:2.
- At the appointed time, it shall speak (come to life) to you as you continue to develop it, until one day you will realize you are not only running with the idea, you are flying with it.

Connect With People of Like Minds

More often than not, we see birds flying in groups. They do this for a number of beneficial reasons:

- For aerodynamics, which allows them to use the air in the most energy efficient way.

- For warmth in wintertime, sharing the benefit of communal warmth to survive severely cold temperatures.

- For foraging, which allows many birds to take advantage of the same food supplies.

- For protection, a larger group of birds has a better chance of spotting a predator or another potential threat compared to a single bird.

All these contribute to the birds achieving great goals with minimal effort because the effort is communal. In studying the behaviour of birds, we can see that connecting with people of like minds and passions, makes it easier to accomplish feats that would otherwise be very difficult to accomplish.

It is a waste of time to try to recreate what has already been created; getting information, connecting with mentors and learning from people who have accomplished what you are trying to do reduces preparation time, and highlights mistakes to avoid. Before you realize it, you are no longer flapping your wings you have started to glide upwards.

There are many groups and organizations in your area of interest you can join as you try to establish yourself. The Internet and other social media outlets are great tools to be familiar with and get connected to others. In the age of technology, everything you need is at the click of a button.

Action Items:

- List the people in your circle and objectively rate how much value they add to you on a daily basis.

- Track this for one month, the result will provide

you with a decent way to gauge whether the others in the group are pulling you down (crab mentality) or enhancing you.

Empower The Leader In You

To soar to your God-ordained potential, you must become relevant in your field and to become relevant you must become a problem solver. People will not listen to you unless you have something to offer. It is what you have to offer that will announce you to the world and keep you at the top. The Bible says,

> [16] A man's gift makes room for him
> And brings him before great men.
>
> *Proverbs 18:16 (NASB)*

However, in order to remain relevant, you must be prepared for unforeseen circumstances that can arise out of the blues. You must know what to do in situations that come your way, as the scout motto says "Be Prepared". Since you cannot predict the future or know what will hit you and when; you must learn to prepare, equip and empower yourself ahead of time. You must strengthen the leader qualities in you.

Like the eagle, you must be able to soar above problems (storms) by developing good problem solving skills.

One of my favourite authors is John Maxwell, the renowned speaker on leadership and the application of its principles to life issues. He has utilized his books and other writings to make leadership issues relevant such that anyone can identify with his ideas and easily apply them to real life situations.

John Maxwell defines a problem as a situation that is counter to our intentions and expectations. Some of the key things to remember according to Maxwell are:

- Life is not problem free – it will always occur
- Each problem is unique and you must handle it with care and courage
- You must see problem as an opportunity to grow or to refine your leadership, therefore, acknowledge it and own it in order to have a solution
- If you can't do something about an issue, it is not your problem, it is a fact of life. Don't expend energy on it.
- Have a mind-set that is not problem focused but is solution focused.

As noted earlier, the eagle thrives well in storms as it uses the strong winds in the storm to propel itself higher above the storms. Problems can be equated with the generation of a hot environment around us that makes us uneasy and uncomfortable. In order to get out of that uncomfortable situation (problem) the tendency to run and make hash and irrational decisions becomes a form of escape from the situation. It is not necessarily the best option, if you are to soar, being a problem solver could create a lift that will make you rise higher than others.

You must learn, equip and develop your mindset to remain calm, bring order into the situation and make recommendations that solves the problem. As you operate in this fashion, people will gradually start to notice that quality as a value you bring to the table or situations you find yourself in. You will find that you are called upon or invited to be part of solution-focused and problem solving teams. This exposure invariably becomes a lifestyle into personal issues that positions you to ride above problems or storms.

"One can never consent to creep when one feels an impulse to soar"
Helen Keller

POINTS TO REMEMBER

1. The creative nature of God in you comes with the ability to produce different things, taking ideas and transforming them into reality.

2. When you process an idea in your mind, a mental picture is formed. This picture registers and takes root. It becomes the driving force that galvanizes the push and passion to pursue the idea.

3. God carefully and quietly hides His most precious gifts so we may experience the joy of discovering them.

4. Embrace your God-directed thoughts, don't push them away because your brain says it is too challenging.

5. Connecting with people of like minds and passion makes it easier to accomplish feats that would otherwise be very difficult to accomplish.

6. Learn to prepare, equip and empower yourself ahead of time. You must strengthen the leader qualities in you.

ACTION ITEMS

- Honestly assess whether you tend to run away from problems, avoid or confront issues and problems.

- Running away or avoiding issues do not develop you. Recognize it and start to strive towards handling issues in a way that makes you grow.

- If you believe you make efforts to confront it, make sure you are using appropriate strategies to resolve problems around you. You should feel some peace at the end of an issue.

- Assess all that went down, the how, where, what and with whom in resolving the issues.

Chapter 7
EMPOWERED LIFESTYLE

As you continue to soar, there will be bumps in the way, turbulence in the air, storms and torrential rains that can stall the upward thrust but you can keep soaring higher with a lifestyle that supports the upward thrust. Much has been written about what helps the eagle soar above storms, why the eagle is the only bird that can stare into the sun and not be blinded by it, that is, do the impossible and yet live.

The expanded and contemporary definitions provided by authors *Robbins, Chatterjee and Canda (1998)*, describe empowerment as "The process by which individuals and groups gain power, access to resources and control over their lives. In doing so, they gain the ability to achieve their highest personal and collective aspirations and goals."

With the right empowerment, you can go beyond your natural strength. You need some sort of power that enables you to achieve the not so ordinary things. It is not so surprising then that the word 'power' is centrally located in the word 'em<u>power</u>ment' *(underlined for emphasis)*.

Empowered living means different things in different situations but for our purposes, it reflects living a life that is guided by excellent qualities, values and lifestyles.

The following qualities, values and lifestyles are

important as we journey through life and different nests. They are characteristics that have set great people aside and if you make them a part of your journey will impact you positively, maintain the rise upwards and sustain you at that higher level.

Life of Integrity and Character

Integrity is one quality that tends to elude most people and yet is seen as very important in various relationships you will pass through. It is demonstrated through complete devotion to keeping one's word.

Who you are, in your heart, is evidenced by what you do on a day-to-day basis, especially when you are pushed into a position where you have to make a choice between two values or alternatives. We must remember that the higher we go, the more others around us will take notice and watch and match our words with our actions. There must be consistency in what we do in public as well as in private. If people do not see all, our God sees in secret.

We read in the following passage, how Samuel was confident in how he lived his life that he challenged people to speak up against him if he cheated them in any way.

> [2] ....I have served as your leader from the time I was a boy to this very day. [3] Now testify against me in the presence of the LORD and before his anointed one. Whose ox or donkey have I stolen? Have I ever cheated any of you? Have I ever oppressed you? Have I ever taken a bribe and perverted justice? Tell me and I will make right whatever I have done wrong."
> [4] "No," they replied, "you have never cheated or oppressed us, and you have never taken even a single bribe."
>
> *1 Samuel 12:2c-4 (NLT)*

Character is who you are when no one is there to observe you. It is a pattern of behavior, thoughts and feelings based on universal principles, moral strength, and integrity (*Ctrs.org*). Developing your character involves defining the boundaries that you will not cross. Character in life is what makes people believe in you and assist you as you go higher in life. Others must be able to trust you, this way they can stand by you as you navigate through the storms, challenges and oppositions as you continue your climb up. We know that our God is trustworthy, He does not lie according to His word and He does not change.

> [6] "*I am the LORD, and I do not change...* "
>
> *Malachi 3:6 (NLT)*

Let this character be found in us as we strive for the highest.

Life of Accountability

Accountability is when you take absolute responsibility for your actions. The final decision to leave the nest should be yours, but you want to be answerable to God who made it possible, those who encouraged you along the way and yourself with the attitude and mindset of "I Can". You want to be accountable also to beneficiaries of your 'new' you, your customers or ministry partners. To soar and reach your goal, accountability is a must have asset that once acquired becomes an indispensable tool for your ascent in life. A mentor or a coach can hold your hand as you assess your performance and the new lifestyle to match your new level. They will help validate your thoughts, ideas, your progress and successes; their input in your life is of great value to you and these are people you don't want to disappoint.

In all, your ultimate accountability is to God.

> [12] *Yes, each of us will give a personal account to God*
>
> **Romans 14:12 (NLT)**

Life of Focus and Order

Once you are out of the nest living a life of focus and order stems from cultivating the ability to identify what is important, zeroing in on the issue and giving it your undivided attention.

Many people are distracted, which resembles the disorder, the chattering and market noise typical in the Nest. They have so many things they want to do but are not sure where to start, how to start and do not know how to prioritize. We live in a world full of distractions and unprofitable activities and as such it is paramount to focus on things that matter in your ascent to your God-ordained height.

If you study the lives of successful people, you will discover that what most people find to be pleasurable and entertaining have no place on their to-do list. They focus mainly on things that matter to their purpose in life; they live in the society but have created their own universe where life is solely driven by their goals and dreams.

Unfortunately, you will observe that for the majority, people around them do not provide the right examples that will positively impact them. Instead, our classrooms, workplaces, and neighborhoods are filled with those who are unable to develop their ideas or complete a creative work because they are too distracted and lack focus and order in their lives. An experience of success in what you have focused on and poured your energy into will spur you on to know the power of focus. A constant reminder is not to remove our eyes away from God and His precepts, so we can reach our heights.

> [112] I am determined to keep your decrees to the very end.
> **Psalm 119:112 (NLT)**
>
> [2] We do this by keeping our eyes on Jesus, the champion who initiates and perfects our faith...
> **Hebrews 12:2 (NLT)**

Time Management

This is an important skill you need to learn if you want to leave the nest to soar. Be a respecter of time. It is God-given. Once lost, it cannot be taken back.

> [15] See then that ye walk circumspectly, not as fools, but as wise,
> [16] Redeeming the time, because the days are evil.
> **Ephesians 5:15-16**

According to Wikipedia, the free online dictionary, "time management is the act or process of planning and exercising conscious control over the amount of time spent on specific activities, especially to increase effectiveness, efficiency or productivity".

"Give whatever you are doing and whoever you are the gift of your attention". Jim Rohn

---

Without good time management you give yourself over to coincidences, you waste time on what is not important or relevant to where God wants you to be. Some leave the nest to soar and achieve greater heights within a short time, others leave the nest at the same time but soar one mile up and dip two miles down. Inability to manage your time on a daily basis, can result in the up today and down tomorrow experience.

Planned and Challenged Life

> [23] The steps of a good man are ordered by the LORD: and he delighteth in his way.
>
> **Psalm 37:23**

As the eagle methodically builds its nest, life is not to be lived haphazardly, it is to be planned and structured. The most important ingredient in living a well planned and focused life is to put God in the center on the spiritual level and on the physical level, to have good health through a healthy lifestyle. *Proverbs 3 verse 6 says, "In all your ways acknowledge Him and He shall direct your paths."*

Commit your life and ways into the hands of God, take time to identify patterns and habits that hinder you from soaring and rising to your God-ordained height. Do not live a defeatist average life or constantly use the statement, 'I am managing' to describe your situation. The instruction or command in the Word of God is that we dominate and not manage. Let God be the center of your life and He will lead you out of the nest so you can continue to soar to higher levels.

Health and Wellness

> [2] Beloved, I pray that in all respects you may prosper and be in good health, just as your soul prospers.
>
> **2 John 1:2 (NASB)**

Your health and the practice of wellness is very important to add to the equation of an empowered lifestyle. You need good health to be of sound mind, to reason, plan and implement all that will assist you to leave the nest for your next level.

Wellness is making healthy food choices, physical exercise a habit, taking time out to enjoy life, being happy and making these practices a daily lifestyle. Wellness includes reaching out and understanding your mental, physical and spiritual health and taking actions to take care of all these levels. At the Empowerment Forum monthly meetings which was the platform to share most of the writings in this book, we identify and discuss issues that impact or enhance the physical and spiritual health of women in particular.

Making little changes in any unhealthy lifestyle you practice is tantamount to the small steps you take as you step out of the nest on your own or nudged out of the nest.

We have empowered you with this chapter so you can look at the spiritual, day-to-day qualities and lifestyle practices that are pathways so you do not return to the nest. Remember, you have left the nest so, keep soaring or if on your way out, walk in the 'I can do' mind frame and sustain it.

POINTS TO REMEMBER

1. Empowered living means different things in different situations but for our purposes, it reflects living a life that is guided by excellent qualities, values and lifestyles.

2. Character in life is what makes people believe in you and assist you as you go higher in life.

3. We live in a world full of distractions and unprofitable activities and as such, it is paramount to focus on things that matter in your ascent to your God-ordained height.

4. The most important ingredient in living a well planned and focused life is to put God in the center on the spiritual level and on the physical level, to have good health through a healthy lifestyle.

5. Do not live a defeatist average life or constantly use the statement, 'I am managing' to describe your situation.

6. You need good health to be of sound mind, to reason, plan and implement all that will, assist you to leave the nest for your next level.

DECLARATION STATEMENT:
"I declare….."

Chapter 8
STOP, LOOK AND LISTEN [SLL]

In or Out of the Nest

This final chapter is included to help you walk through that last part that might still nudge at you of what else to do.

At times you might have said, I have done all, learnt new skills in the physical, in the spiritual you have prayed, fasted, sown a seed. You have acquired the highest degrees in your area of interest. If you have done all these, the natural tendency is for you to give up, and continue to justify remaining in the nest, it's somewhat of a natural reaction. But have you given thought to one more thing, the need to understand and differentiate between what God alone can do and where your own effort stops? We noted earlier being nudged out of the nest by God himself through His Spirit that He has sent to us. This chapter is an attempt to pull together what is termed "SLL", as other things you might want to do.

Let's look at what SLL stands for.

'STOP' means to discontinue something; to cease doing something, or make somebody cease doing something. It could infer that one come to a standstill, or bring something to a standstill.

You might be at the point where you need to Stop all the hustling as the Lord might be saying, **"BE STILL"**. Moses had to Stop and look at the burning bush in order to receive the directives and strategies that he would use against Pharaoh.

> [1] Now Moses was tending the flock of Jethro his father-in-law, the priest of Midian, and he led the flock to the far side of the wilderness and came to Horeb, the mountain of God. [2] There the angel of the LORD appeared to him in flames of fire from within a bush. Moses saw that though the bush was on fire it did not burn up. [3] So Moses thought, "I will go over and see this strange sight—why the bush does not burn up."
> [4] When the LORD saw that he had gone over to look, God called to him from within the bush, "Moses! Moses!"
> And Moses said, "Here I am."
> [5] "Do not come any closer," God said. "Take off your sandals, for the place where you are standing is holy ground."
>
> *Exodus 3:1-5 (NIV)*

Jesus stopped for blind Bartholomew so the miracle of sight could be performed.

It might be time to change strategy but you cannot hear the instruction to change strategy because you have continued your headlong push. It might require a conscious effort of putting aside that planning until there is clarity in your thoughts. Remember, to rely on divine guidance from the Holy Spirit.

'**LOOK**', for our purposes in this book is to ascertain by the use of both the spiritual and physical eyes to assess the current position of things. This means you constantly scan your environment. You ask questions like, 'where am I in the journey to get to the next level?' Am I still stuck in the nest or I am out but fluttering my wings to know how high I am on the way up. 'How do I take the bitterness out of my life and ensure I am not sinking into depression nor groaning about things out of my control'? Realizing that when you live in bitterness, it's negative energy that saps strength out and though out of the nest, you have not soared high but on the reverse, you are diving downwards.

In *Genesis 13 verse 10*, Lot took a long look at the fertile plains and moved there. He lost out in the end, as what was once fertile became charred land because of the destruction by God.

In *Genesis 13 verse 14*, Abraham was instructed by God of how to do his looking, he was told to "look as far as he can see in every direction, north and south, east and west." Lot, on the other hand, only saw in one direction.

Elisha prayed that the eyes of his servant Gehazi be opened so he could look at the heavenly hosts who were more than the military contingent sent to arrest him by the king of Samaria.

> [15] When the servant of the man of God got up and went out early the next morning, an army with horses and chariots had surrounded the city. "Oh no, my lord! What shall we do?" the servant asked.
> [16] "Don't be afraid," the prophet answered. "Those who are with us are more than those who are with them."
> [17] And Elisha prayed, "Open his eyes, LORD, so that he may see." Then the LORD opened the servant's eyes, and he looked and saw the hills full of horses and chariots of fire all around Elisha
>
> *2 Kings 6:15-17 (NIV)*

So, when you are looking, you will need to look through many lenses in order to capture what needs to be fixed, changed or redesigned in order to bring out the best, leave the nest and start to soar. You should not be too busy and lose cognizance of what is going on around you. May our spiritual and physical eyes be open to look and see.

The last component after we have Stopped and Looked by checking out our surrounding is to **'LISTEN'**.

Listening is defined as making a conscious effort to hear: to concentrate on hearing somebody or something; to pay attention; or be involved in reflecting, clarifying and summarizing what one has heard.

At this phase, you might receive suggestions, attend various discussion groups, seminars, workshops but you must set time aside to reflect, clarify, and understand the journey of your life. Whether you are in or out of the nest, your comfort zone, you want to periodically take time out to Stop, identify and acknowledge which bus stop you are. Look and examine what is happening around so you know you are still going in the right direction.

Finally, Listen so as to make informed decisions. If you are still in the nest, your informed decision gleaned from information shared with you or directives from God can assist you in stepping out. If you are out of the nest, the decision will assist you to start the process to go forward and soar for the limit is no longer the sky but beyond as well.

POINTS TO REMEMBER

1. Giving thought to one more thing, the need to understand and differentiate between what God alone can do and where your own effort stops.

2. It might be time to change strategy but you cannot hear the instruction to change strategy because you have continued your head long push.

3. Remember, to rely on divine guidance from the Holy Spirit.

4. When you are looking, you will need to look through many lenses in order to capture what needs to be fixed, changed or redesigned in order to bring out the best, leave the nest and start to soar

I pray as you finish reading this book, you have been able to glean ideas and strategies with an understanding to leave the nest to soar. I hope you have also been encouraged and empowered to rise and shine. That's where you belong and that's where you will be.

We hope we have, in the words of *Hebrews 10 verse 24*, demonstrated to you, our love to you to go after your purpose and soar as you are destined.

> [24] Let us think of ways to motivate one another to acts of love and good works.
>
> *Hebrews 10:24 (NLT)*

As this book goes to print, I thank God that I am leaving one nest, the Health Program where I worked as Project Director in the last three years out of the nine plus years that I worked with the Program. I am soaring to another level and joining the ranks of published authors.

If this book has blessed you, share it with friends and families. No one should be left behind from fulfilling God's ordained purpose and the creative potentials that will make us Soar. **Leave the Nest to Soar.**

You can too!

References

1. On Character (2016). www.citrs.org/character
2. Gasset, Jose Ortega y - http://www.brainyquote.com/quotes/authors/j/jose_ortega_y_gasset.html
3. Helen Keller quotes http://www.brainyquote.com/quotes/authors/h/helen_keller.html
4. Keller, Helen. https://en.wikipedia.org/wiki/Helen_Keller
5. Ladd, Karol (2014). Positive Leadership Principles for Women. 8 secrets to Inspire and Impact everyone around you.
6. Maxwell, John C. Problems. "This article is used by permission from GiANT Impact. Find other leadership content, resources, training, and events at www.giantimpact.com."
7. John C. Maxwell, (2013). The value of appreciating Problems. http://www.johnmaxwell.com/blog/the-value-of-appreciating-problems. Accessed July 15, 2016.
8. Maxwell, John C (2015). Wisdom from Women in the Bible. Giants of the Faith Speak into our Lives. FaithWords.
9. Nest definition, DICTIONARY.COM.
10. Robbins Susan, Chatterjee, Pranab, Canda, R Edward (1998). Contemporary Human Behavior Theory: A Critical perspective for Social Work. Boston: Allyn & Bacon.
11. Rohn, Jim - http://www.great-quotes.com/quotes/author/Jim/Rohn/pg/3.
12. Selwyn Hughes (2010) Every Day with Jesus. "Soaring above the Storm".
13. Selwyn Hughes, (2001). The Divine Eagle published by CWR.
14. Lester Sumrall Evangelical Association (1982). The Gifts and Ministries of the Holy Spirit. Updated edition. Whitetaker House, PA.

Bible References

All references are from the King James Version except where indicated

Chapter 1
Exodus 16:9-18
Exodus 16: 35
Exodus 17:2-6
Exodus 13: 21-22
Deuteronomy. 29:5
Psalms. 105:37
Matthew 19:12 (NKJV)

Chapter 2
1 Corinthians. 2:9
Jeremiah 29:11
Revelations 5:11-14
Deuteronomy 32:11
Deuteronomy 32:11 (NLT- 2nd version used for emphasis)

Chapter 3
Deuteronomy 1:6-7 (NLT)
Deuteronomy 31:6 (NLT)
Matthew 28:20
Genesis 32:22-30
Jonah 1:1-14
Genesis 12:1-8
Isaiah 40:31 (NLT)

Chapter 4
Exodus 19:3-6 (NIV)
1 Peter 2:9
Luke 4:18
1 John 3:8
Luke 1:8-17
Matthew 3:13-17
Isaiah 40:21

Genesis 1:1-2 (NLT)
1 Samuel 10:5-6 (NLT)
Matthew 1:20c (NLT)
Matthew 3:16 (NLT)
Romans 8:11 (NLT)
Acts 2:4 (NLT)

Chapter 5
Genesis 1:28
Deuteronomy 32:8-14
Esther 9:32 (NLT)

Chapter 6
Isaiah 40: 31 (NLT)
Exodus 31: 1-5 (NIV)
Exodus. 36:1
Proverbs. 23:7
Genesis 15: 1-6
Romans 4: 20-21
Proverbs 25:2
Isaiah 42:16 (NLT)
Luke 9:62
Proverbs 18: 16 (NASB)

Chapter 7
1 Samuel 12:2c-4 (NLT)
Malachi 3:6 (NLT)
Romans 14:12 (NLT)
Psalms 119:112 (NLT)
Hebrews 12:2 (NLT)
Ephesians 5:15-16
Psalms 37:23
Proverbs 3: 6 (NKJV)
3 John 2 (NASB)

Chapter 8
Exodus 3: 1-5 (NIV)
2 Kings 6:15-17 (NIV)
Hebrews 10:24 (NLT)

www.ingramcontent.com/pod-product-compliance
Lightning Source LLC
Chambersburg PA
CBHW032149040426
42449CB00005B/455